easy

Desserts

easy

Desserts

MARKS &
SPENCER

Marks and Spencer p.l.c.
PO Box 3339
Chester CH99 9QS

shop online
www.marksandspencer.com

Designed by Mark Cavanagh
Cover and additional photography by Charlie Richards*
Additional food styling by Mary Wall
Introduction by Anne Sheasby

ISBN: 978-1-84805-022-8

Printed in China

The views expressed in this book are those of the author but they are general views only and readers
are urged to consult a relevant and qualified specialist for individual advice in particular situations.
Marks and Spencer p.l.c. and Exclusive Editions hereby exclude all liability to the extent permitted by
law for any errors or omissions in this book and for any loss, damage or expense (whether direct or
indirect) suffered by a third party relying on any information contained in this book.

NOTES FOR THE READER
This book uses both metric and imperial measurements. Follow the same units of measurement
throughout; do not mix metric and imperial. All spoon measurements are level, unless otherwise
stated: teaspoons are assumed to be 5 ml and tablespoons are assumed to be 15 ml. Unless otherwise
stated, milk is assumed to be semi-skimmed, eggs and individual vegetables such as potatoes are
medium, and pepper is freshly ground black pepper. Recipes using raw or very lightly cooked eggs
should be avoided by infants, the elderly, pregnant women, convalescents and anyone suffering from
an illness. The times given are an approximate guide only.

*pages 11, 14, 19, 20, 29, 31, 37, 53, 54, 57, 60, 63, 65, 66, 69, 72, 77, 93, 95, 99, 101, 102, 105, 107, 108, 113, 117, 125, 127, 131, 133, 137, 139, 140 and 149.

Contents

Introduction

A delicious dessert provides the perfect finale to many meals and offers a tempting sweet treat that so many of us enjoy.

Desserts vary enormously and they don't have to be indulgent to be enjoyable. You may prefer to choose a rich and creamy concoction or a chocolate-laden creation, but on other occasions you may favour a lighter or more fruity combination. While a crème brûlèe, trifle or other cream-based dessert will satisfy that craving for something sweet, a simple fruit salad or compote provides a light and refreshing end to a meal.

Desserts to Suit all Occasions

Many different desserts, both hot and cold, can be created from the wide range of ingredients that are readily available to us, providing the perfect conclusion to many meals. Make the most of fruits and other ingredients in season, when they are in prime condition and at their most abundant, to create some really scrumptious desserts.

Fruit desserts, pies, flans and pastries, batter puddings, creamy desserts and cheesecakes, mousses and jellies, meringues, ices and iced desserts, and so on, provide plenty of choice to suit all occasions. Perhaps you are planning a dessert for a family meal, a mid-week supper for two, an informal get-together with friends, a buffet or a sophisticated dinner party, or maybe you are simply someone who wants to satisfy their sweet tooth.

Selecting Which Type of Dessert to Make

It is important to consider the rest of the meal when choosing a dessert and to pick a dessert that balances well with, and complements, the other dishes being served. The occasion, the number of people you are serving, the preparation time you have available and the time of year are all important aspects to consider when selecting a dessert.

For example, a hot pudding would not be the most popular choice to present to guests on a scorching summer's day. Instead, serve a cold perhaps fruit-based dessert, such as a chilled cheesecake, soufflé or fruit mousse on a hot day, and save the old favourites such as pies, crumbles and other baked puddings for cheering up those crisp autumn or chilly winter days.

Other factors to consider include whether or not you decide to offer a choice and serve more than one dessert to your guests. Perhaps, rather than presenting the dessert in one large serving dish, you may choose to make individual portions (these are especially good for dinner parties). Also bear in mind how easy the dessert will be to serve and if it can be cut into portions beforehand to make it easier to dish up at the table. Think about whether the dessert can be prepared in advance or if it may need some last-minute attention – if so, how does this fit with the occasion and the time available?

Decorating Desserts

A simple decoration is often all that is needed to ensure a dessert is as pleasing to the eye as it is to the palate. Fresh fruits make an easy and attractive decoration for many desserts, especially fresh berries such as strawberries (used whole, halved or sliced into fan shapes) or raspberries, small sprigs of red or white currants or a cluster of cherries.

A scattering of seeds or whole, flaked or chopped toasted nuts provides a decorative touch as well as adding texture, flavour and colour. A simple dusting of sifted icing sugar or cocoa powder can provide the perfect finish. Edible flowers (such as pansies, roses and nasturtiums) or small sprigs or leaves of fresh herbs (such as mint or lemon balm) can transform a dessert.

Frosted fruits such as grapes, small berries or cherries (dipped in egg white and caster sugar, then left to dry), frosted leaves or flowers, or chocolate-dipped fruits provide a lovely finishing touch. Citrus fruit slices or twists, or curls of thinly pared citrus zest create an effective, delicate decoration.

Last but by no means least, chocolate provides the perfect decoration for numerous desserts. Grated chocolate, chocolate curls, scrolls, ruffles, leaves or lacy lattices, or a drizzle of melted chocolate will transform the simplest of desserts into something really impressive.

Serving Desserts

Many desserts are best served simply on their own, but some are made even more appealing when served with, for example, a homemade biscuit, wafer, brandy snap or amaretti biscuit, a scoop or two of ice cream or sorbet, a dollop of whipped cream, Greek yogurt or crème fraîche, or a spoonful or two of hot custard. Simple sweet sauces, fruit coulis or fruit purées also add that extra finishing flair to a variety of desserts.

Pies &
Pastries

Apple Pie

serves 6

pastry

350 g/12 oz plain flour

pinch of salt

85 g/3 oz butter or margarine, cut into small pieces

85 g/3 oz lard or white vegetable fat, cut into small pieces

about 6 tbsp cold water

beaten egg or milk, for glazing

filling

750 g–1 kg/1 lb 10 oz–2 lb 4 oz cooking apples, peeled, cored and sliced

125 g/4½ oz soft light brown or caster sugar, plus extra for sprinkling

½–1 tsp ground cinnamon, mixed spice or ground ginger

1–2 tbsp water (optional)

To make the pastry, sift the flour and salt into a mixing bowl. Add the butter and fat and rub it in with your fingertips until the mixture resembles fine breadcrumbs. Add the water and gather the mixture together into a dough. Wrap the dough in clingfilm and chill in the refrigerator for 30 minutes.

Preheat the oven to 220°C/425°F/Gas Mark 7. Roll out almost two thirds of the pastry thinly and use to line a deep 23-cm/9-inch pie dish.

To make the filling, mix the apples with the sugar and spice and pack into the pastry case; the filling can come up above the rim. Add the water if needed, particularly if the apples are not very juicy.

Roll out the remaining pastry to form a lid. Dampen the edges of the pie rim with water and position the lid, pressing the edges firmly together. Trim and crimp the edges.

Use the trimmings to cut out leaves or other shapes to decorate the top of the pie; dampen and attach. Glaze the top of the pie with beaten egg or milk, make 1 or 2 slits in the top and place the pie on a baking sheet.

Bake in the preheated oven for 20 minutes, then reduce the temperature to 180°C/350°F/Gas Mark 4 and bake for a further 30 minutes, or until the pastry is a light golden brown. Serve hot or cold, sprinkled with sugar.

Lemon Meringue Pie

serves 4

pastry

200 g/7 oz plain flour, plus extra for dusting

100 g/3½ oz butter, diced, plus extra for greasing

50 g/1¾ oz icing sugar, sifted

finely grated rind of 1 lemon

1 egg yolk, beaten

3 tbsp milk

filling

3 tbsp cornflour

300 ml/10 fl oz cold water

juice and grated rind of 2 lemons

175 g/6 oz caster sugar

2 eggs, separated

To make the pastry, sift the flour into a large bowl and rub in the butter. Then mix in the remaining ingredients. Knead briefly on a lightly floured work surface. Wrap the dough in clingfilm and leave to rest for 30 minutes.

Preheat the oven to 180°C/350°F/Gas Mark 4. Grease a 20-cm/8-inch ovenproof flan dish with butter.

Roll out the pastry to a thickness of 5 mm/¼ inch and line the dish with it. Prick with a fork, then line with greaseproof paper and fill with baking beans. Bake for 15 minutes. Remove from the oven, then reduce the oven temperature to 150°C/300°F/Gas Mark 2.

To make the filling, mix the cornflour with a little water to make a paste. Pour the remaining water into a saucepan. Stir in the lemon juice and rind and cornflour paste. Bring to the boil, while stirring, and cook for 2 minutes. Cool slightly, then stir in 5 tablespoons of the sugar and the egg yolks and pour into the pastry case.

In a separate bowl, whisk the egg whites until stiff. Gradually whisk in the remaining sugar and spread over the pie.

Bake for 40 minutes, until the meringue is light brown, and serve warm.

Banoffee Toffee Pie

serves 4

2 x 400 ml/14 fl oz cans sweetened condensed milk

6 tbsp butter, melted, plus extra for greasing

150 g/5½ oz digestive biscuits, crushed into crumbs

50 g/1¾ oz almonds, toasted and ground

50 g/1¾ oz hazelnuts, toasted and ground

4 ripe bananas

1 tbsp lemon juice

1 tsp vanilla essence

75 g/2¾ oz chocolate, grated

450 ml/16 fl oz thick double cream, whipped

Place the cans of condensed milk in a large saucepan and cover them with water. Bring to the boil, then reduce the heat and simmer for 2 hours. Ensure the water is topped up regularly with boiling water to keep the cans covered. Carefully lift out the hot cans and leave to cool.

Preheat the oven to 180°C/350°F/Gas Mark 4. Grease a 23-cm/9-inch loose-bottomed flan tin with butter. Place the remaining butter in a bowl and add the biscuits and nuts. Mix together well, then press the mixture evenly into the base and sides of the tin. Bake for 10–12 minutes, then remove from the oven and leave to cool.

Peel and slice the bananas and place them in a bowl. Sprinkle over the lemon juice and vanilla essence and mix gently. Spread the banana mixture over the biscuit crust in the tin, then open the cans of condensed milk and spoon the contents over the bananas. Sprinkle over 50 g/1¾ oz of the chocolate, then top with a thick layer of whipped cream. Scatter over the remaining chocolate and serve.

Mississippi Mud Pie

serves 6

pastry

225 g/8 oz plain flour, plus extra for dusting

2 tbsp cocoa powder

140 g/5 oz butter, diced

2 tbsp caster sugar

1–2 tbsp cold water

filling

175 g/6 oz butter

350 g/12 oz soft dark brown sugar

4 eggs, lightly beaten

4 tbsp cocoa powder, sifted

150 g/5½ oz plain chocolate

300 ml/10 fl oz single cream

1 tsp chocolate essence

to decorate

425 ml/15 fl oz double cream, whipped

chocolate flakes and curls

To make the pastry, sift the flour and cocoa powder into a mixing bowl. Rub in the butter with your fingertips until the mixture resembles fine breadcrumbs. Stir in the sugar and enough cold water to mix to a soft dough. Wrap the dough in clingfilm and chill in the refrigerator for 15 minutes.

Preheat the oven to 190°C/375°F/Gas Mark 5. Roll out the pastry on a lightly floured work surface and use to line a 23-cm/9-inch loose-based flan tin. Line with baking paper and fill with baking beans. Bake in the preheated oven for 15 minutes. Remove the paper and beans from the pastry case and cook for a further 10 minutes until crisp.

To make the filling, beat the butter and sugar together in a bowl and gradually beat in the eggs with the cocoa powder. Melt the chocolate in a heatproof bowl set over a pan of simmering water, then cool slightly. Beat it into the mixture with the single cream and the chocolate essence.

Reduce the oven temperature to 160°C/325°F/Gas Mark 3. Pour the mixture into the pastry case and bake for 45 minutes, or until the filling has set.

Let the mud pie cool completely, then transfer it to a serving plate, if you like. Cover with the whipped cream. Decorate the pie with chocolate flakes and curls and then chill until ready to serve.

Pumpkin Pie

serves 6

1.8 kg/4 lb sweet pumpkin

55 g/2 oz cold unsalted butter, diced, plus extra for greasing

140 g/5 oz plain flour, plus extra for dusting

¼ tsp baking powder

1½ tsp ground cinnamon

¾ tsp ground nutmeg

¾ tsp ground cloves

1 tsp salt

50 g/1¾ oz caster sugar

3 eggs

400 ml/14 fl oz can sweetened condensed milk

½ tsp vanilla essence

1 tbsp demerara sugar

streusel topping

2 tbsp plain flour

4 tbsp demerara sugar

1 tsp ground cinnamon

2 tbsp cold unsalted butter, in small pieces

75 g/2¾ oz shelled pecan nuts, chopped

75 g/2¾ oz shelled walnuts, chopped

Preheat the oven to 190°C/375°F/Gas Mark 5. Halve the pumpkin. Remove and discard the seeds, stem and stringy insides. Put the pumpkin halves, face down, in a shallow baking tin and cover with foil. Bake for 1½ hours then leave to cool.

Scoop out the flesh, mash in a large bowl, and drain away any excess liquid. Cover and chill until ready to use.

To make the pastry, first grease a 23-cm/9-inch round pie dish with butter. Sift the flour and baking powder into a large bowl. Stir in ½ tsp cinnamon, ¼ tsp nutmeg, ¼ tsp cloves, ½ tsp salt and all the caster sugar. Rub in the butter with your fingertips until the mixture resembles fine breadcrumbs, then make a well in the centre. Lightly beat 1 egg and pour it into the well. Mix together until a soft dough is formed. Roll out the pastry on a lightly floured surface and use to line the pie dish, trimming the edges. Cover and chill in the refrigerator for 30 minutes.

Preheat the oven to 220°C/425°F/Gas Mark 7. To make the filling, stir the condensed milk and remaining eggs into the pumpkin purée. Add the remaining spices and salt, then stir in the vanilla essence and demerara sugar. Pour into the pastry case and bake for 15 minutes.

Meanwhile, make the topping. Combine the flour, sugar and cinnamon in a bowl, rub in the butter until crumbly, then stir in the nuts. Remove the pie from the oven and reduce the heat to 180°C/350°F/Gas Mark 4. Sprinkle the topping over the pie, then bake for a further 35 minutes. Serve hot or cold.

Tarte au Citron

serves 6

pastry

200 g/7 oz plain flour, plus extra for dusting

3 tbsp ground almonds

100 g/3½ oz butter, diced, plus extra for greasing

50 g/1¾ oz icing sugar, sifted

finely grated rind of 1 lemon

1 egg yolk, beaten

3 tbsp milk

filling

4 eggs

250 g/9 oz caster sugar

juice and finely grated rind of 2 lemons

150 ml/5 fl oz double cream

mascarpone cheese or crème fraîche and fresh raspberries, to serve

To make the pastry, sift the flour into a bowl. Mix in the almonds, then rub in the butter. Mix in the icing sugar, lemon rind, egg yolk and milk. Knead briefly on a lightly floured work surface, then leave to rest for 30 minutes.

Preheat the oven to 180°C/350°F/Gas Mark 4. Grease a 23-cm/9-inch flan tin with butter. Roll out the pastry to a thickness of 5 mm/¼ inch and use to line the base and sides of the tin. Prick all over with a fork, line with greaseproof paper and fill with baking beans. Bake for 15 minutes.

Remove from the oven. Reduce the oven temperature to 150°C/300°F/Gas Mark 2.

To make the filling, crack the eggs into a bowl. Whisk in the sugar, then the lemon juice and rind and cream. Spoon into the pastry case and bake for 45 minutes. Remove from the oven and leave to cool. Serve the tart topped with mascarpone or crème fraîche and fresh raspberries.

Paper-thin Fruit Pies

makes 4

1 dessert apple

1 ripe pear

2 tbsp lemon juice

55 g/2 oz butter

4 sheets filo pastry, thawed if frozen

2 tbsp apricot jam

1 tbsp orange juice

1 tbsp chopped pistachio nuts

2 tsp icing sugar, for dusting

Preheat the oven to 200°C/400°F/Gas Mark 6.

Core and thinly slice the apple and pear and immediately toss them in the lemon juice to prevent them from turning brown.

Melt the butter in a saucepan over a low heat. Cut each sheet of pastry into 4 and cover with a clean, damp tea towel. Brush a 4-cup non-stick muffin tin (cup size 10 cm/4 inches in diameter) with a little of the butter.

Working on each pie separately, brush 4 small sheets of pastry with butter. Press a sheet of pastry into the base of 1 cup. Arrange the other sheets of pastry on top at slightly different angles. Repeat with the other sheets of pastry to make another 3 pies.

Arrange the apple and pear slices alternately in the centre of each pie case and lightly crimp the edge of the pastry.

Stir the jam and orange juice together until smooth and brush over the fruit. Bake in the preheated oven for 12–15 minutes. Sprinkle with the pistachio nuts, dust lightly with icing sugar and serve hot straight from the oven.

Maple Pecan Pies

makes 12

pastry

140 g/5 oz plain flour, plus
extra for dusting

85 g/3 oz butter, cut into
small pieces

55 g/2 oz golden caster
sugar

2 egg yolks

filling

2 tbsp maple syrup

150 ml/5 fl oz double cream

115 g/4 oz golden caster
sugar

pinch of cream of tartar

6 tbsp water

115 g/4 oz shelled pecan
nuts, chopped

12–24 pecan nut halves,
to decorate

Preheat the oven to 200°C/400°F/Gas Mark 6.

To make the pastry, sift the flour into a mixing bowl and rub in the butter with your fingertips until the mixture resembles breadcrumbs. Add the sugar and egg yolks and mix to form a soft dough. Wrap the dough in clingfilm and chill in the refrigerator for 30 minutes.

On a lightly floured work surface, roll out the pastry thinly. Cut out 12 circles and use to line 12 tartlet tins. Prick the bases with a fork. Line each tin with baking paper and fill with baking beans. Bake in the preheated oven for 10–15 minutes until light golden. Remove the paper and beans and bake for a further 2–3 minutes. Leave to cool on a wire rack.

Mix half the maple syrup and half the cream in a bowl. Put the sugar, cream of tartar and water in a saucepan and heat gently until the sugar dissolves. Bring to the boil and boil until light golden. Remove from the heat and stir in the maple syrup and cream mixture.

Return the saucepan to the heat and cook to the soft ball stage (116°C/240°F): that is, when a little of the mixture dropped into a bowl of cold water forms a soft ball of toffee. Stir in the remaining cream and leave until cool. Brush the remaining maple syrup over the edges of the pies. Put the chopped pecan nuts in the pastry cases and spoon in the toffee. Top each pie with 1 or 2 pecan halves. Leave to cool completely before serving.

Chocolate Blueberry Pies

makes 10

200 g/7 oz blueberries

2 tbsp crème de cassis

10 g/¼ oz icing sugar, sifted

pastry

175 g/6 oz plain flour

40 g/1½ oz cocoa powder

55 g/2 oz caster sugar

pinch of salt

125 g/4½ oz butter, cut into small pieces

1 egg yolk

1–2 tbsp cold water

filling

140 g/5 oz plain chocolate

225 ml/8 fl oz double cream

150 ml/5 fl oz soured cream or crème fraîche

To make the pastry, put the flour, cocoa, sugar and salt in a large bowl and rub in the butter until the mixture resembles breadcrumbs. Add the egg and a little cold water to form a dough. Wrap the dough in clingfilm and chill in the refrigerator for 30 minutes. Remove the dough from the refrigerator and roll out. Use to line ten 10-cm/4-inch tartlet cases. Freeze for 30 minutes.

Preheat the oven to 180°C/350°F/Gas Mark 4. Bake the cases in the oven for 15–20 minutes. Leave to cool.

Put the blueberries, cassis and icing sugar in a saucepan and warm through so that the berries become shiny but do not burst. Leave to cool.

To make the filling, melt the chocolate in a heatproof bowl set over a pan of simmering water, then cool slightly. Whip the double cream until stiff and fold in the soured cream and melted chocolate.

Transfer the tartlet cases to a serving plate and divide the chocolate filling among them, smoothing the surface with a palette knife, then top with the blueberries.

Custard Tart

serves 8

pastry

150 g/5½ oz plain flour, plus extra for dusting

25 g/1 oz caster sugar

125 g/4½ oz butter, diced

1 tbsp water

filling

3 eggs

150 ml/5 fl oz single cream

150 ml/5 fl oz milk

freshly grated nutmeg

fresh strawberries, to serve

To make the pastry, place the flour and sugar in a large bowl and rub in the butter with your fingertips until the mixture resembles breadcrumbs.

Add the water and mix together to form a soft dough. Wrap in clingfilm and leave to chill in the refrigerator for 30 minutes.

Roll out the dough on a lightly floured work surface to form a round, slightly larger than a 24-cm/9½-inch loose-bottomed flan tin, then use to line the tin. Prick the dough with a fork and leave to chill for 30 minutes.

Preheat the oven to 190°C/375°F/Gas Mark 5. Line the pastry case with foil and baking beans and bake in the preheated oven for 15 minutes. Remove the foil and baking beans and bake the pastry case for a further 15 minutes.

To make the filling, whisk the eggs, cream, milk and nutmeg together. Pour the filling into the prepared pastry case. Return the tart to the oven and cook for 25–30 minutes, or until just set. Serve with the fresh strawberries.

Crème Brûlée Tarts

serves 6

pastry

150 g/5½ oz plain flour, plus extra for dusting

25 g/1 oz caster sugar

125 g/4½ oz butter, cut into small pieces

1 tbsp water

filling

4 egg yolks

50 g/1¾ oz caster sugar

400 ml/14 fl oz double cream

1 tsp vanilla essence

demerara sugar, for sprinkling

To make the pastry, place the flour and sugar in a bowl and rub in the butter with your fingers until the mixture resembles fine breadcrumbs. Add the water and work the mixture together until a soft dough has formed. Wrap in clingfilm and leave to chill for 30 minutes.

Roll out the dough on a lightly floured work surface and use to line six 10-cm/4-inch tart tins. Prick the base with a fork and leave to chill for 20 minutes.

Preheat the oven to 190°C/375°F/Gas Mark 5. Line the pastry cases with foil and baking beans and bake in the oven for 15 minutes. Remove the foil and beans and cook for a further 10 minutes until crisp and golden. Leave to cool.

Meanwhile, make the filling. In a bowl, beat the egg yolks and caster sugar until thick and pale. Heat the cream with the vanilla essence in a saucepan until just below boiling point, then pour it onto the egg mixture, whisking constantly.

Return the mixture to a clean saucepan and bring to just below boiling point, stirring, until thick. Do not boil or it will curdle.

Leave the mixture to cool slightly, then pour it into the tart cases. Leave to cool and then leave to chill overnight.

Preheat the grill to medium. Sprinkle the tarts with demerara sugar. Place under the hot grill for a few minutes

Summer Fruit Tartlets

makes 12

pastry

200 g/7 oz plain flour, plus extra for dusting

85 g/3 oz icing sugar

55 g/2 oz ground almonds

115 g/4 oz unsalted butter, diced and chilled

1 egg yolk

1 tbsp milk

filling

275 g/9¾ oz cream cheese

icing sugar, to taste, plus extra for dusting

350 g/12 oz fresh summer berries and currants, such as blueberries, raspberries, small strawberries, redcurrants and whitecurrants, picked over and prepared

To make the pastry, sift the flour and sugar into a bowl, then stir in the almonds. Rub in the butter with your fingertips until the mixture resembles breadcrumbs. Add the egg yolk and milk and mix to form a dough. Turn out on to a lightly floured surface and knead briefly. Wrap the dough in clingfilm and chill in the refrigerator for 30 minutes.

Preheat the oven to 200°C/400°F/Gas Mark 6. Roll out the pastry and use it to line 12 deep tartlet or individual brioche tins. Prick the pastry bases with a fork. Press a piece of foil into each tartlet, covering the edges, and bake in the preheated oven for 10–15 minutes, or until light golden brown. Remove the foil and bake for a further 2–3 minutes. Transfer the pastry cases to a wire rack to cool.

To make the filling, mix the cream cheese and icing sugar together in a bowl. Put a spoonful of filling in each pastry case and arrange the fruit on top. Dust with sifted icing sugar and serve immediately.

Truffled Honey Tart

serves 6

pastry

125 g/4½ oz plain flour, plus extra for dusting

pinch of salt

75 g/2½ oz cold butter, cut into pieces

1 tsp icing sugar

cold water

filling

250 g/9 oz curd cheese

100 g/3½ oz cream cheese

125 ml/4 fl oz double cream

2 egg yolks, plus 1 whole egg

25 g/1 oz caster sugar

4 tbsp flower honey, plus extra for drizzling

crystallized violets or sugared rose petals, to decorate

Lightly butter a 22-cm/9-inch loose-bottomed fluted tart tin. Sift the flour and salt into a food processor, add the butter and process until the mixture resembles fine breadcrumbs. Tip the mixture into a large bowl, add the sugar and a little cold water, just enough to bring the dough together. Turn out on to a surface dusted with more flour and roll out the pastry 8 cm/3¼ inches larger than the tin. Carefully lift the pastry into the tin and press to fit. Roll the rolling pin over the tin to neaten the edges and trim the excess pastry. Fit a piece of baking paper into the tart case, fill with baking beans and chill in the refrigerator for 30 minutes. Meanwhile, preheat the oven to 190°C/375°F/Gas Mark 5.

Remove the pastry case from the refrigerator and bake blind for 10 minutes in the preheated oven, then remove the beans and paper and bake for a further 5 minutes.

Mix the curd cheese, cream cheese and cream together until smooth then stir in the egg yolks and whole egg plus the sugar and honey until completely smooth. Pour into the pastry case and bake for 30 minutes. Remove from the oven and cool in the tin for 10 minutes. Drizzle with more honey and decorate with violets or petals.

Baklava

serves 4–6

150 g/5½ oz shelled pistachio nuts, finely chopped

75 g/2¾ oz toasted hazelnuts, finely chopped

75 g/2¾ oz blanched hazelnuts, finely chopped

grated rind of 1 lemon

1 tbsp brown sugar

1 tsp ground mixed spice

250 g/9 oz (about 16 sheets) frozen filo pastry, thawed if frozen

150 g/5½ oz butter, melted, plus extra for greasing

250 ml/9 fl oz water

2 tbsp clear honey

1 tbsp lemon juice

300 g/10½ oz caster sugar

½ tsp ground cinnamon

Preheat the oven to 160°C/325°F/Gas Mark 3. Grease a round cake tin, 18 cm/7 inches in diameter and 5 cm/ 2 inches deep, with butter. Place the nuts, lemon rind, sugar and mixed spice in a bowl and mix well.

Cut the whole stack of filo sheets to the size of the tin. Keep the filo rounds covered with a damp tea towel. Lay 1 round on the base of the tin and brush with melted butter. Add another 6 rounds on top, brushing between each layer with melted butter. Spread over one-third of the nut mixture, then add 3 rounds of buttered filo. Spread over another third of nut mixture then top with 3 more rounds of buttered filo. Spread over the remaining nut mixture and add the last 3 rounds of buttered filo. Cut into wedges, then bake in the oven for 1 hour.

Meanwhile, place the water, honey, lemon juice, caster sugar and cinnamon in a saucepan. Bring to the boil, stirring. Reduce the heat and simmer, without stirring, for 15 minutes. Cool.

Remove the baklava from the oven, pour over the syrup and leave to set before serving.

Chocolate Filo Parcels

makes 18

55 g/2 oz plain chocolate, broken into pieces

85 g/3 oz ground hazelnuts

1 tbsp finely chopped fresh mint

125 ml/4 fl oz soured cream

2 dessert apples

9 sheets filo pastry, about 15 cm/6 inches square, thawed if frozen

55–85 g/2–3 oz butter, melted

icing sugar, for dusting

Preheat the oven to 190°C/375°F/Gas Mark 5.

Melt the chocolate in a heatproof bowl set over a saucepan of gently simmering water. Remove from the heat and leave to cool slightly.

Mix together the hazelnuts, mint and soured cream in a bowl. Peel the apples and grate them into the bowl, then stir in the melted chocolate and mix well.

Cut each sheet of filo pastry into 4 squares. Keep the squares you are not using covered with a damp cloth. Brush 1 square with melted butter, place a second square on top and brush with melted butter. Place a tablespoonful of the chocolate mixture in the centre, then bring up the corners of the squares and twist together to enclose the filling completely. Continue making parcels in the same way until you have used up all the pastry and filling.

Brush a baking sheet with melted butter and place the parcels on it. Bake for about 10 minutes until crisp and golden. Leave to cool slightly, then dust with icing sugar and serve.

Pear & Pecan Strudel

serves 4

2 ripe pears

55 g/2 oz butter

55 g/2 oz fresh white breadcrumbs

55 g/2 oz shelled pecan nuts, chopped

25 g/1 oz light muscovado sugar

finely grated rind of 1 orange

100 g/3½ oz filo pastry sheets, thawed if frozen

6 tbsp orange blossom honey

2 tbsp orange juice

icing sugar, for dusting

Greek-style yogurt, to serve (optional)

Preheat the oven to 200°C/400°F/Gas Mark 6.

Peel, core and chop the pears. Melt 1 tablespoon of the butter in a frying pan and gently fry the breadcrumbs until golden. Transfer to a bowl and add the pears, nuts, muscovado sugar and orange rind. Put the remaining butter in a small saucepan and heat until melted.

Reserve 1 sheet of filo pastry, keeping it well wrapped, and brush the remaining filo sheets with a little melted butter. Spoon a little of the nut filling onto the first filo sheet, leaving a 2.5-cm/1-inch margin around the edge. Build up the strudel by placing buttered filo sheets on top of the first, spreading each one with nut filling as you build up the layers. Drizzle the honey and orange juice over the top.

Fold the short ends over the filling, then roll up, starting at a long side. Carefully lift onto a baking sheet, with the seam on top. Brush with any remaining melted butter and crumple the reserved sheet of filo pastry around the strudel. Bake for 25 minutes, or until golden and crisp. Dust with icing sugar and serve warm with Greek-style yogurt, if using.

Chocolate Nut Strudel

serves 6

150 g/5½ oz butter, preferably unsalted, plus extra for greasing

200 g/7 oz mixed chopped nuts

115 g/4 oz plain chocolate, chopped

115 g/4 oz milk chocolate, chopped

115 g/4 oz white chocolate, chopped

200 g/7 oz filo pastry, thawed if frozen

3 tbsp golden syrup

55 g/2 oz icing sugar

Preheat the oven to 190°C/375°F/Gas Mark 5.

Lightly grease a baking sheet with butter. Reserve 1 tablespoon of the nuts. Place the remaining nuts in a bowl and mix together with the 3 types of chocolate.

Place 1 sheet of filo pastry on a clean tea towel. Melt the butter and use it to brush the sheet of filo. Drizzle the filo with a little syrup and sprinkle with some nuts and chocolate. Place another sheet of filo on top and repeat until you have used all the nuts and chocolate.

Use the tea towel to help you carefully roll up the strudel and place on the baking sheet, drizzle with a little more syrup and sprinkle with the reserved nuts.

Bake for 20-25 minutes. If the nuts start to brown too much, cover the strudel with a sheet of foil. Sprinkle the strudel with icing sugar, slice and serve warm.

Chocolate Eclairs

makes 12
choux pastry

70 g/2½ oz butter, cut into small pieces, plus extra for greasing

150 ml/5 fl oz water

100 g/3½ oz plain flour, sifted

2 eggs

pastry cream

2 eggs, lightly beaten

4 tbsp caster sugar

2 tbsp cornflour

300 ml/10 fl oz milk

¼ tsp vanilla essence

icing

2 tbsp butter

1 tbsp milk

1 tbsp cocoa powder

55 g/2 oz icing sugar

50 g/1¾ oz white chocolate, broken into pieces

Preheat the oven to 200°C/400°F/Gas Mark 6. Lightly grease a baking sheet.

Place the water in a saucepan, add the butter and heat gently until the butter melts. Bring to a rolling boil, then remove the saucepan from the heat and add the flour all at once, beating well until the mixture leaves the sides of the saucepan and forms a ball. Leave to cool slightly, then gradually beat in the eggs to form a smooth, glossy mixture. Spoon into a large piping bag fitted with a 1-cm/½-inch plain nozzle.

Sprinkle the baking sheet with a little water. Pipe éclairs 7.5 cm/3 inches long, spaced well apart. Bake for 30–35 minutes, or until crisp and golden. Make a small slit in the side of each éclair to let the steam escape. Leave to cool on a wire rack.

Meanwhile, make the pastry cream. Whisk the eggs and sugar until thick and creamy, then fold in the cornflour. Heat the milk until almost boiling and pour onto the eggs, whisking. Transfer to the saucepan and cook over a low heat, stirring until thick. Remove the saucepan from the heat and stir in the vanilla essence. Cover with baking paper and leave to cool.

To make the icing, melt the butter with the milk in a saucepan. Remove from the heat and stir in the cocoa and sugar. Split the éclairs lengthways and pipe in the pastry cream. Spread the icing over the top of the éclairs. Melt a little white chocolate in a heatproof bowl set over a saucepan of gently simmering water, then drizzle over the chocolate icing and leave to set. Serve immediately.

Profiteroles

serves 6

choux pastry

5 tbsp butter, plus extra for greasing

200 ml/7 fl oz cold water

100 g/3½ oz plain flour

3 eggs, beaten

cream filling

300 ml/10 fl oz double cream

3 tbsp caster sugar

1 tsp vanilla essence

chocolate & brandy sauce

125 g/4½ oz plain dark chocolate, broken into pieces

2½ tbsp butter

6 tbsp water

2 tbsp brandy

Preheat the oven to 200°C/400°F/Gas Mark 6. Grease a large baking sheet with butter.

To make the pastry, place the water and butter in a saucepan and bring to the boil. Meanwhile, sift the flour into a bowl. Remove the saucepan from the heat and beat in the flour until smooth. Cool for 5 minutes. Beat in enough of the eggs to give the mixture a soft, dropping consistency. Transfer to a piping bag fitted with a 1-cm/ ½-inch plain nozzle. Pipe small balls onto the baking sheet. Bake for 25 minutes. When removed from the oven, pierce each ball with a skewer in order to let steam escape.

To make the filling, whip together the cream, sugar and vanilla essence. Cut the pastry balls almost in half, then fill with cream.

To make the sauce, gently melt the chocolate and butter with the water in a small saucepan, stirring until smooth. Stir in the brandy. Pile the profiteroles into individual serving dishes or into a pyramid on a raised cake stand. Pour over the sauce and serve.

Cakes &
Bakes

Black Forest Gâteau

serves 8

3 tbsp butter, melted, plus extra for greasing

900 g/2 lb fresh cherries, stoned and halved

250 g/9 oz caster sugar

100 ml/3½ fl oz cherry brandy

100 g/3½ oz plain flour

50 g/1¾ oz cocoa powder

½ tsp baking powder

4 eggs

1 litre/1¾ pints double cream

to decorate

plain chocolate, grated

fresh cherries, whole

Preheat the oven to 180°C/350°F/Gas Mark 4. Grease and line a 23-cm/9-inch springform cake tin.

Place the cherries in a saucepan and add 3 tablespoons of the sugar and the cherry brandy. Simmer for 5 minutes. Drain, reserving the syrup. In another bowl, sift together the flour, cocoa and baking powder.

Place the eggs in a heatproof bowl and beat in 160 g/5¾ oz of the sugar. Place the bowl over a saucepan of simmering water and beat for 6 minutes, or until thickened. Remove from the heat, then gradually fold in the flour mixture and melted butter. Spoon into the cake tin and bake for 40 minutes then let cool.

Turn out the cake and cut in half horizontally. Mix the cream and the remaining sugar together and whip lightly. Spread the reserved syrup over the cut sides of the cake, then top with a layer of cream. Arrange the cherries over one half of the cake, then place the other half on top of it. Cover the whole cake with cream, press grated chocolate all over the surface and decorate with whole fresh cherries.

Mocha Layer Cake

serves 8

butter, for greasing

250 g/9 oz self-raising flour

¼ tsp baking powder

4 tbsp cocoa powder

115 g/4 oz caster sugar

2 eggs

2 tbsp golden syrup

150 ml/5 fl oz sunflower oil

150 ml/5 fl oz milk

filling and topping

1 tsp instant coffee powder

1 tbsp boiling water

300 ml/10 fl oz double cream

2 tbsp icing sugar

to decorate

50 g/1¾ oz chocolate shavings

icing sugar, for dusting

Preheat the oven to 180°C/350°F/Gas Mark 4. Lightly grease three 18-cm/7-inch shallow cake tins.

Sift the flour, baking powder and cocoa powder together into a large bowl. Stir in the caster sugar then make a well in the centre. Add the eggs, syrup, oil and milk to the well and gradually beat in with a wooden spoon to form a smooth mixture. Divide between the prepared tins.

Bake in the preheated oven for 35–45 minutes, or until springy to the touch. Leave to cool slightly in the tins, then transfer to a wire rack and leave to cool completely.

To make the filling, dissolve the coffee in the boiling water and put in a bowl with the cream and icing sugar. Whip until the cream is just holding its shape. Use half the cream to sandwich the 3 cakes together. Spread the remaining cream over the top and side of the cake.

To decorate, lightly press the chocolate shavings into the cream around the side of the cake. Transfer to a serving plate. Cut a few thin strips of baking paper and arrange on top of the caraque. Dust lightly with icing sugar, then carefully remove the paper.

Sachertorte

serves 10

175 g/6 oz continental plain chocolate, broken into pieces

140 g/5 oz butter, preferably unsalted, plus extra for greasing

140 g/5 oz caster sugar

6 eggs, separated

175 g/6 oz plain flour

fresh strawberries, to serve

icing & filling

225 g/8 oz continental plain chocolate, broken into pieces

5 tbsp cold strong black coffee

115 g/4 oz icing sugar, sifted

6 tbsp good-quality apricot jam, warmed

Preheat the oven to 150°C/ 300°F/Gas Mark 2. Grease and base-line a 23-cm/9-inch round springform cake tin.

Melt the chocolate for the main cake in a heatproof bowl set over a saucepan of barely simmering water. Cream the butter and 70 g/2½ oz of the caster sugar in a bowl until pale and fluffy. Add the egg yolks and beat well. Add the melted chocolate in a thin stream, beating well. Sift the flour, then fold into the mixture. Whisk the egg whites in a separate large, clean bowl until soft peaks form. Add the remaining caster sugar and whisk until stiff and glossy. Fold half into the chocolate mixture, then fold in the remainder.

Spoon into the prepared tin and smooth the surface. Bake in the preheated oven for 1–1¼ hours, or until a skewer inserted into the centre comes out clean. Leave the cake to cool slightly in the tin, then transfer to a wire rack and leave to cool completely.

To make the icing, melt 175 g/6 oz of the chocolate in a heatproof bowl set over a saucepan of barely simmering water. Beat in the coffee. Whisk into the icing sugar in a bowl to form a thick icing. Cut the cake horizontally in half. Sandwich the layers together with the jam. Invert the cake onto a wire rack. Spoon over the icing and spread to coat the top and side. Leave to set for 5 minutes, letting any excess drip through the rack. Transfer to a serving plate and leave to set for at least 2 hours.

Melt the remaining chocolate and spoon into a piping bag fitted with a fine plain nozzle. Pipe 'Sachertorte' on the cake top and leave to set. Serve with fresh strawberries.

White Truffle Cake

serves 12

butter, for greasing

50 g/1¾ oz white chocolate

2 eggs

50 g/1¾ oz caster sugar

70 g/2½ oz plain flour

for the truffle topping

300 ml/10 fl oz double cream

350 g/12 oz white chocolate, broken into pieces

250 g/9 oz mascarpone cheese

50 g/1¾ oz white chocolate shavings

Preheat the oven to 180°C/ 350°F/Gas Mark 4. Grease and base-line a 20-cm/8-inch round springform cake tin. Melt the white chocolate in a heatproof bowl set over a saucepan of barely simmering water.

Using a hand-held electric whisk, beat the eggs and sugar together in a large bowl until thick and pale – the mixture should leave a trail when the whisk is lifted. Sift the flour and gently fold into the eggs with a metal spoon or palette knife. Add the melted chocolate. Pour the mixture into the prepared tin and bake in the preheated oven for 25 minutes, or until springy to the touch. Leave to cool slightly in the tin, then transfer to a wire rack and leave to cool completely. Return the cold cake to the tin.

To make the topping, put the cream in a saucepan and bring to the boil, stirring constantly. Leave to cool slightly, then add the white chocolate and stir until melted and combined. Remove from the heat and set aside until almost cool, stirring, then mix in the mascarpone cheese. Pour on top of the cake. Chill in the refrigerator for 2 hours.

To decorate, pick up the shavings carefully and arrange on the top of the dessert. Serve immediately.

Chocolate Fudge Gâteau

serves 10

1 tsp sunflower oil, for oiling

85 g/3 oz plain chocolate

225 g/8 oz butter, softened

225 g/8 oz light muscovado sugar

4 eggs, beaten

225 g/8 oz self-raising flour

55 g/2 oz ground almonds

1–2 tbsp cooled, boiled water

115 g/4 oz soft vanilla fudge, diced

icing

175 g/6 oz butter, softened

280 g/10 oz icing sugar, sifted

3–4 tbsp single cream

55 g/2 oz light muscovado sugar

1 tbsp cocoa powder, sifted

to decorate

55 g/2 oz plain chocolate, grated

cocoa powder-dusted truffles

Preheat the oven to 180°C/350°F/Gas Mark 4. Lightly oil and base-line two 20-cm/8-inch shallow cake tins with non-stick baking paper. Melt the chocolate in a heatproof bowl set over a saucepan of barely simmering water. Cream the butter and muscovado sugar together in a bowl until light and fluffy, then gradually add the eggs, beating well and adding a little of the flour after each addition. Gently fold in the melted chocolate and then the remaining flour until combined. Stir in the ground almonds with 1–2 tablespoons of cooled boiled water. Mix to form a soft dropping consistency. Stir in the fudge pieces, then divide between the prepared cake tins and smooth the surfaces.

Bake in the preheated oven for 35–40 minutes, or until springy to the touch. Leave the cakes to cool slightly in the tins, then transfer to a wire rack and leave to cool completely.

To make the icing, beat the butter in a bowl until soft and creamy, then gradually beat in the icing sugar, adding a little of the cream as the mixture becomes stiff. Add the muscovado sugar with the cocoa powder and gently stir. Stir in sufficient of the remaining cream to give a soft, spreadable icing. Put the grated chocolate on a sheet of non-stick baking paper. Cut the cakes horizontally in half and sandwich together with one-third of the icing. Spread another third around the side, then roll the cake in the grated chocolate. Transfer to a serving plate. Spread the top with the remaining icing, piping some around the outside edge for an attractive finish. Decorate with the truffles before serving the gâteau.

Devil's Food Cake

serves 6

100 g/3½ oz plain
chocolate, broken into
pieces

325 g/11½ oz self-raising
flour

1 tsp bicarbonate of soda

225 g/8 oz butter, plus extra
for greasing

500 g/1 lb 2 oz soft
light brown sugar

1 tsp vanilla extract

3 eggs

125 ml/4 fl oz buttermilk

200 ml/7 fl oz boiling water

crystallized orange rind,
to decorate

icing

225 g/8 oz caster sugar

2 egg whites

1 tbsp lemon juice

3 tbsp orange juice

Preheat the oven to 190°C/375°F/Gas Mark 5. Grease and base-line two 20-cm/8-inch shallow cake tins. Melt the chocolate in a heatproof bowl set over a saucepan of barely simmering water. Sift the flour and bicarbonate of soda together into a bowl.

Cream the butter and sugar together in a separate bowl until pale and fluffy. Beat in the vanilla extract and the eggs, one at a time, beating well after each addition. Add a little flour if the mixture starts to curdle.

Fold the melted chocolate into the mixture until well blended. Gradually fold in the remaining flour, then stir in the buttermilk and boiling water.

Divide the mixture between the prepared tins and smooth the surfaces. Bake in the preheated oven for 30 minutes, or until springy to the touch. Leave the cakes to cool slightly in the tins, then transfer to a wire rack and leave to cool completely.

Put all the icing ingredients in a large heatproof bowl set over a saucepan of gently simmering water. Using a hand-held electric whisk, beat until thick and soft peaks form. Remove from the heat and beat until cool.

Sandwich the cakes together with some of the icing. Swirl the remainder over the top of the cake. Decorate with crystallized orange rind.

Raspberry Dessert Cake

serves 8–10

250 g/9 oz plain chocolate, broken into pieces

225 g/8 oz unsalted butter, plus extra for greasing

1 tbsp strong, dark coffee

5 eggs

100 g/3½ oz golden caster sugar

85 g/3 oz plain flour

1 tsp ground cinnamon

175 g/6 oz fresh raspberries, plus extra to serve

icing sugar, for dusting (optional)

whipped cream, to serve

Preheat the oven to 160°C/325°F/Gas Mark 3. Grease a 23-cm/9-inch cake tin and line the base with non-stick baking paper. Put the chocolate, butter and coffee in a small, heatproof bowl. Set over a saucepan of barely simmering water and heat until melted. Remove from the heat, stir and leave to cool slightly.

Beat the eggs and caster sugar together in a separate bowl until pale and thick. Gently fold in the chocolate mixture.

Sift the flour and cinnamon into another bowl, then fold into the chocolate mixture. Pour into the prepared tin and sprinkle the raspberries evenly over the top.

Bake in the preheated oven for about 35–45 minutes, or until the cake is well risen and springy to the touch. Leave to cool in the tin for 15 minutes before turning out onto a large serving plate. Dust with icing sugar, if using, before serving with extra fresh raspberries and whipped cream.

Strawberry Cheesecake

serves 8

base

55 g/2 oz butter, preferably unsalted

200 g/7 oz crushed digestive biscuits

85 g/3 oz chopped walnuts

filling

450 g/1 lb mascarpone cheese

2 eggs, beaten

3 tbsp caster sugar

250 g/9 oz white chocolate, broken into pieces

300 g/10½ oz strawberries, hulled and quartered

topping

175 g/6 oz mascarpone cheese

50 g/1¾ oz white chocolate shavings

4 strawberries, halved

Preheat the oven to 150°C/300°F/Gas Mark 2. Melt the butter in a saucepan over a low heat and stir in the crushed biscuits and nuts. Spoon into a 23-cm/9-inch round springform cake tin and press evenly over the base with the back of a spoon. Set aside.

To make the filling, beat the mascarpone cheese in a bowl until smooth, then beat in the eggs and sugar. Melt the white chocolate in a heatproof bowl set over a saucepan of barely simmering water, stirring until smooth. Remove from the heat and leave to cool slightly, then stir into the cheese mixture. Stir in the strawberries.

Spoon the mixture into the cake tin, spread out evenly and smooth the surface. Bake in the preheated oven for 1 hour, or until the filling is just firm. Turn off the oven and leave the cheesecake to cool inside with the door slightly ajar until completely cold. Transfer to a serving plate.

For the topping, spread the mascarpone cheese on top. Decorate with the chocolate shavings and the strawberry halves.

Chocolate Panforte

serves 4–6

100 g/3½ oz candied orange peel

50 g/1¾ oz dried apricots, chopped

2 tbsp orange-flavoured liqueur, such as Cointreau

100 g/3½ oz shelled whole hazelnuts

150 g/5½ oz split almonds, toasted

100 g/3½ oz plain flour

2 tbsp unsweetened cocoa powder

2 tsp mixed spice

125 g/4½ oz caster sugar

150 ml/5 fl oz clear honey

icing sugar and sprigs of mint, to decorate

Preheat the oven to 150°C/300°F/Gas Mark 2. Line a 20-cm/8-inch round cake tin.

Put the orange peel, apricots and liqueur into a heatproof bowl and leave to soak. Toast the hazelnuts under a preheated medium grill until the skins split. Remove to a clean tea towel and rub to remove the skins. Coarsely chop, then add to the fruit with the almonds and mix well.

Sift the flour, cocoa powder and mixed spice into a separate bowl, then mix into the fruit and nuts. Bring the sugar and honey to the boil in a saucepan over a low heat, stirring. Continue to boil, stirring, for 5 minutes, then quickly pour the syrup over the fruit and nuts and mix well. Turn into the prepared tin and level the surface. Bake in the oven for 50 minutes.

Remove from the oven, turn out onto a wire rack and discard the lining paper. Leave to cool, then dredge with icing sugar. Serve immediately, decorated with sprigs of mint, or store for up to 3–4 months in an airtight container.

Hot Chocolate Soufflés with Coffee Sabayon

serves 6

butter, for greasing

55 g/2 oz golden caster sugar, plus extra for coating

3 tbsp cornflour

250 ml/9 fl oz milk

115 g/4 oz plain chocolate, broken into pieces

4 eggs, separated

coffee sabayon

2 eggs

3 egg yolks

85 g/3 oz golden caster sugar

4 tsp instant coffee granules

2 tbsp brandy

icing sugar, for dusting

Preheat the oven to 190°C/375°F/Gas Mark 5. Grease 6 medium-sized ramekins with butter and coat with caster sugar. To make the soufflés, place the cornflour in a bowl. Add a little milk and stir until smooth. Pour the remaining milk into a heavy-based saucepan and add the chocolate. Heat gently until the chocolate has melted, then stir. Pour the chocolate milk onto the cornflour paste, stirring. Return to the pan and bring to the boil, stirring. Simmer for 1 minute. Remove from the heat and stir in the egg yolks, one at a time. Cover and cool slightly.

Place the egg whites in a large, spotlessly clean, greasefree bowl and whisk until beginning to stand in soft peaks. Gradually whisk in the caster sugar until stiff but not dry. Stir a little of the meringue into the chocolate mixture, then carefully fold in the remainder. Pour into the prepared ramekins and bake in the preheated oven for 25–30 minutes, or until the soufflés are well risen and wobble slightly when pushed.

Just before the soufflés are ready, make the coffee sabayon. Place all the ingredients in a heavy-based saucepan. Place the saucepan over a very low heat and whisk constantly, until the mixture is thick and light. Dust a little icing sugar over the soufflés and serve immediately, with the sabayon.

Rich Ginger Brownies with Port Cream

makes 8

175 g/6 oz unsalted butter, plus extra for greasing

200 g/7 oz plain chocolate

200 g/7 oz granulated sugar

4 eggs, beaten

2 tsp vanilla extract

1 tbsp stem ginger syrup

100 g/3½ oz plain flour

55 g/2 oz preserved stem ginger in syrup, chopped

port cream

200 ml/7 fl oz ruby port

200 ml/7 fl oz double cream

1 tbsp icing sugar

1 tsp vanilla extract

25 g/1 oz chopped crystallized ginger, to decorate

Preheat the oven to 180°C/350°F/Gas Mark 4. Grease a 23-cm/9-inch square shallow baking tin.

Place the chocolate and butter in a saucepan and heat gently, stirring, until melted. Remove from the heat and stir in the sugar.

Beat the eggs, vanilla extract and ginger syrup into the chocolate mixture. Stir in the flour and stem ginger, mixing evenly.

Pour the mixture into the prepared tin and bake in the oven for 30–35 minutes, until just firm to the touch.

Meanwhile, make the port cream. Place the port in a saucepan and simmer over a medium-high heat until reduced to about 4 tablespoons. Cool. Whip the cream until beginning to thicken, then beat in the sugar, reduced port and vanilla extract, continuing to whip until it holds soft peaks.

Remove the tin from the oven. Cool for 2–3 minutes in the tin, then cut into 8 triangles. Place on individual serving plates and add a spoonful of port cream to each. Top with pieces of crystallised ginger and serve warm.

Individual Chocolate Puddings

serves 4

puddings

100 g/3½ oz caster sugar

3 eggs

75 g/2¾ oz plain flour, sifted

50 g/1¾ oz cocoa powder, sifted

100 g/3½ oz unsalted butter, melted, plus extra for greasing

100 g/3½ oz plain chocolate, melted

chocolate sauce

2 tbsp unsalted butter

100 g/3½ oz plain chocolate

5 tbsp water

1 tbsp caster sugar

1 tbsp coffee-flavoured liqueur, such as Kahlúa

coffee beans, to decorate

To make the puddings, put the sugar and eggs into a heatproof bowl and place over a saucepan of simmering water. Whisk for about 10 minutes until frothy. Remove the bowl from the heat and fold in the flour and cocoa powder. Fold in the butter, then the chocolate. Mix well.

Grease 4 small pudding basins with butter. Spoon the mixture into the basins and cover with greaseproof paper. Top with foil and secure with string. Place the puddings in a large saucepan filled with enough simmering water to reach halfway up the sides of the basins. Steam for about 40 minutes or until cooked through.

About 2–3 minutes before the end of the cooking time, make the sauce. Put the butter, chocolate, water and sugar into a small saucepan and warm over a low heat, stirring constantly, until melted together. Stir in the liqueur.

Remove the puddings from the heat, turn out into serving dishes and pour over the sauce. Decorate with coffee beans and serve.

Toffee Sponge Cake

serves 4

cake

75 g/2¾ oz sultanas

150 g/5½ oz stoned dates, chopped

1 tsp bicarbonate of soda

2 tbsp butter, plus extra for greasing

200 g/7 oz demerara sugar

2 eggs

200 g/7 oz self-raising flour, sifted

sticky toffee sauce

2 tbsp butter

175 ml/6 fl oz double cream

200 g/7 oz demerara sugar

orange zest, to decorate

freshly whipped cream, to serve

To make the cake, put the fruits and bicarbonate of soda into a heatproof bowl. Cover with boiling water and leave to soak.

Preheat the oven to 180°C/350°F/Gas Mark 4. Grease a round cake tin, 20 cm/8 inches in diameter, with butter.

Put the remaining butter in a separate bowl, add the sugar and mix well. Beat in the eggs then fold in the flour. Drain the soaked fruits, add to the bowl and mix. Spoon the mixture evenly into the prepared cake tin. Transfer to the preheated oven and bake for 35–40 minutes. The cake is cooked when a skewer inserted into the centre comes out clean.

About 5 minutes before the end of the cooking time, make the sauce. Melt the butter in a saucepan over a medium heat. Stir in the cream and sugar and bring to the boil, stirring constantly. Lower the heat and simmer for 5 minutes.

Turn out the cake onto a serving plate and pour over the sauce. Decorate with zested orange rind and serve with whipped cream.

Steamed Syrup Sponge Pudding

serves 6

115 g/4 oz butter, plus extra
for greasing

2 tbsp golden syrup, plus
extra to serve

115 g/4 oz caster sugar

2 eggs, lightly beaten

175 g/6 oz self-raising flour

2 tbsp milk

grated rind of 1 lemon

Butter two 600-ml/1-pint pudding basins and put equal amounts of the syrup into the bottoms.

Beat together the butter and sugar until soft and creamy, then beat in the eggs, a little at a time.

Fold in the flour and stir in the milk to make a soft dropping consistency. Add the lemon rind. Turn equal amounts of the mixture into the pudding basins.

Cover the surfaces with circles of greaseproof or baking paper and top with a pleated sheet of foil. Secure with some string or crimp the edges of the foil to ensure a tight fit around the basins.

Place the puddings in a large saucepan half-filled with boiling water. Cover the saucepan and bring back to the boil over a medium heat. Reduce the heat to a slow simmer and steam for 1½ hours until risen and firm. Keep checking the water level and top up with boiling water as necessary.

Remove the pan from the heat and lift out the pudding basins. Remove the covers and loosen the puddings from the sides of the basins using a knife.

Turn out into a warmed dish and heat a little more syrup to serve with the puddings.

Rice Pudding

serves 4–6

1 tbsp melted butter

115 g/4 oz pudding rice

55 g/2 oz caster sugar

850 ml/1½ pints full-cream milk

½ tsp vanilla extract

40 g/1½ oz unsalted butter

whole nutmeg, for grating

cream, jam, fruit purée, stewed fruit or ice cream, to serve (optional)

Preheat the oven to 300°C/150°F/Gas Mark 2. Grease a 1.2-litre/2-pint baking dish (a gratin dish is good) with the melted butter. Place the rice in the dish and sprinkle with the sugar.

Heat the milk in a saucepan until almost boiling, then pour over the rice. Add the vanilla extract and stir well to dissolve the sugar.

Cut the butter into small pieces and scatter over the surface of the pudding.

Grate the whole nutmeg over the top, using as much as you like to give a good covering.

Place the dish on a baking tray and bake in the centre of the oven for 1½–2 hours until the pudding is well browned on the top. You can stir it after the first half hour to disperse the rice.

Serve hot and, if desired, with some cream, jam, fresh fruit purée, stewed fruit or ice cream. It is also good cold with fresh fruit or honey.

Ginger Baked Alaskas

serves 4

4 tbsp sultanas or raisins

3 tbsp dark rum or ginger wine

4 square slices ginger cake

4 scoops vanilla ice cream or rum and raisin ice cream

3 egg whites

175 g/6 oz granulated or caster sugar

Preheat the oven to 230°C/450°F/Gas Mark 8. Mix the sultanas with the rum in a small bowl.

Place the cake slices well apart on a baking sheet and scatter a spoonful of the soaked sultanas on each slice.

Place a scoop of ice cream in the centre of each slice and place in the freezer.

Meanwhile, whisk the egg whites in a large grease-free bowl until soft peaks form then gradually whisk the sugar into the egg whites, a tablespoonful at a time, until the mixture forms stiff peaks.

Remove the ice cream-topped cake slices from the freezer and spoon the meringue over the ice cream. Spread to cover the ice cream completely.

Bake in the oven for about 5 minutes until starting to brown. Serve immediately.

Queen of Puddings

serves 4–6

2 tbsp butter

600 ml/1 pint milk

115 g/4 oz fresh white breadcrumbs

115 g/4 oz caster sugar

grated rind of 1 lemon

3 eggs, separated

3 tbsp raspberry jam, warmed

1 tsp golden granulated sugar

Preheat the oven to 180°C/350°F/Gas Mark 4. Using a little of the butter, grease a 1-litre/1¾-pint baking dish.

Heat the remaining butter in a saucepan with the milk and gently bring to the boil over a medium heat.

Remove from the heat and stir in the breadcrumbs, 1 tablespoon of the caster sugar and the lemon rind.

Allow to stand and cool for 15 minutes, then beat in the egg yolks.

Pour the mixture into the baking dish, smooth the surface and bake in the centre of the oven for about 30 minutes until it is set. Spread over the jam.

Whisk the egg whites in a grease-free mixing bowl until very thick, then gradually add the remaining caster sugar. Continue whisking until all the sugar has been added.

Spoon the meringue over the pudding and make sure the meringue covers it completely. Swirl the meringue into attractive peaks and sprinkle with the granulated sugar.

Bake again in the centre of the oven for 10–15 minutes until the meringue is golden brown but still soft. Serve warm.

Fruits

Apple & Blackberry Crumble

serves 4

900 g/2 lb cooking apples

300 g/10½ oz blackberries, fresh or frozen

55 g/2 oz light muscovado sugar

1 tsp ground cinnamon

crumble topping

85 g/3 oz self-raising flour

85 g/3 oz wholemeal plain flour

115 g/4 oz unsalted butter, diced

55 g/2 oz demerara sugar

custard or pouring cream, to serve

Preheat the oven to 200°C/400°F/Gas Mark 6. Peel and core the apples, then cut them into chunks. Put them in a bowl with the blackberries, muscovado sugar and cinnamon and mix together, then transfer to an ovenproof baking dish.

To make the crumble topping, sieve the self-raising flour into a bowl and stir in the wholemeal flour. Rub in the butter with your fingertips until the mixture resembles coarse breadcrumbs. Stir in the demerara sugar.

Spread the crumble topping over the fruit and bake in the preheated oven for 40–45 minutes, or until the apples are soft and the crumble is golden brown and crisp. Serve with custard or pouring cream.

Fruit Cobbler

serves 6

900 g/2 lb fresh berries and currants, such as blackberries, blueberries, raspberries, redcurrants and blackcurrants

85–115 g/3–4 oz caster sugar

2 tbsp cornflour

cobbler topping

200 g/7 oz plain flour

2 tsp baking powder

pinch of salt

55 g/2 oz unsalted butter, diced and chilled

2 tbsp caster sugar

175 ml/6 fl oz buttermilk

1 tbsp demerara sugar

single or double cream, to serve

Preheat the oven to 200°C/400°F/Gas Mark 6. Pick over the fruit, mix with the caster sugar and cornflour and put in a 25-cm/10-inch shallow, ovenproof dish.

To make the cobbler topping, sieve the flour, baking powder and salt into a large bowl. Rub in the butter until the mixture resembles breadcrumbs, then stir in the caster sugar. Pour in the buttermilk and mix to a soft dough.

Drop spoonfuls of the dough on top of the fruit roughly, so that it doesn't completely cover the fruit. Sprinkle with the demerara sugar and bake in the preheated oven for 25–30 minutes until the crust is golden and the fruit is tender.

Remove from the oven and leave to stand for a few minutes before serving with cream.

Pears in Wine

serves 4

4 large pears

225 g/8 oz caster sugar

1 cinnamon stick or vanilla pod

150 ml/5 fl oz water

150 ml/5 fl oz red wine

Peel the pears, leaving the stalks intact. Cut a thin slice off the base of each pear so that it will stand upright.

Put the sugar and cinnamon stick in a large saucepan, add the water and bring to the boil over a medium heat, stirring until the sugar has dissolved. Add the pears, reduce the heat, cover and then simmer for 15 minutes.

Pour in the wine and simmer, uncovered, for a further 15 minutes, or until the pears are just tender. Remove the pears with a slotted spoon and stand them in a serving dish.

Remove and discard the cinnamon stick and bring the wine syrup back to the boil. Boil rapidly until thickened, then pour the syrup over the pears and leave to cool. Chill for at least 1 hour before serving.

Flambéed Peaches

serves 4

3 tbsp unsalted butter

3 tbsp muscovado sugar

4 tbsp orange juice

6 peaches, peeled, halved and stoned

2 tbsp almond liqueur or peach brandy

4 tbsp toasted flaked almonds

Heat the butter, muscovado sugar and orange juice in a large, heavy-based frying pan over a low heat, stirring constantly, until the butter has melted and the sugar has dissolved.

Add the peaches and cook for 1–2 minutes on each side, or until golden.

Add the almond liqueur and ignite with a match or taper. When the flames have died down, transfer to serving dishes, sprinkle with toasted flaked almonds and serve immediately.

Banana Fritters

serves 4

70 g/2½ oz plain flour

2 tbsp rice flour

1 tbsp caster sugar

1 egg, separated

150 ml/5 fl oz coconut milk

sunflower oil for
deep-frying

6 large bananas

to decorate

1 tsp icing sugar

1 tsp ground cinnamon

lime wedges

Sift the plain flour, rice flour and sugar into a bowl and make a well in the centre. Add the egg yolk and coconut milk. Beat the mixture until a smooth, thick batter forms.

Whisk the egg white in a clean, dry bowl until stiff enough to hold soft peaks. Fold it into the batter lightly and evenly.

Heat a 6-cm/2½-inch depth of oil in a large saucepan to 180–190°C/350–375°F, or until a cube of bread browns in 30 seconds. Cut the bananas in half crossways, then dip them quickly into the batter to coat them.

Drop the bananas carefully into the hot oil and deep-fry in batches for 2–3 minutes until golden brown, turning once.

Drain on kitchen paper. Sprinkle with icing sugar and cinnamon and serve immediately, with lime wedges for squeezing juice as desired.

Grilled Cinnamon Oranges

serves 4

4 large oranges

1 tsp ground cinnamon

1 tbsp demerara sugar

Preheat the grill to high. Cut the oranges in half and discard any pips. Using a sharp or curved grapefruit knife, carefully cut the flesh away from the skin by cutting around the edge of the fruit. Cut across the segments to loosen the flesh into bite-sized pieces that will spoon out easily.

Place the orange halves, cut-side up, in a shallow, heatproof dish. Mix the cinnamon with the sugar in a small bowl and sprinkle evenly over the orange halves. Cook under the preheated grill for 3–5 minutes, or until the sugar has caramelized and is golden and bubbling. Serve immediately.

Baked Apples

serves 4

4 medium-sized cooking
apples

1 tbsp lemon juice

50 g/1¾ oz blueberries

50 g/1¾ oz raisins

25 g/1 oz chopped, toasted
mixed nuts

½ tsp ground cinnamon

2 tbsp soft brown sugar

275 ml/9½ fl oz red wine

2 tsp cornflour

4 tsp water

double cream, to serve

Preheat the oven to 200°C/400°F/Gas Mark 6. Using a sharp knife, score a line around the centre of each apple. Core the apples, then brush the centres with the lemon juice to prevent discoloration. Transfer them to a small roasting tin.

Place the blueberries and raisins in a bowl, then add the nuts, cinnamon and sugar. Mix together well. Pile the mixture into the centres of the apple, then pour over the wine.

Transfer the stuffed apples to the preheated oven and bake for 40–45 minutes, or until tender. Remove from the oven, then lift the apples out of the roasting tin and keep them warm.

Blend the cornflour with the water, then add the mixture to the cooking juices in the roasting tin. Transfer to the hob and cook over a medium heat, stirring, until thickened. Remove from the heat and pour over the apples. Serve the apples with double cream.

Fruit Pancakes

serves 4

pancakes

125 g/4½ oz plain flour

pinch of salt

2 eggs

300 ml/10 fl oz milk

2–3 tbsp vegetable oil

filling

1 banana

1 tbsp lemon juice

2 nectarines, stoned and cut into small pieces

1 mango, peeled, stoned and cut into small pieces

3 kiwi fruits, peeled and cut into small pieces

2 tbsp maple syrup

icing sugar, to dust

whipped cream, to serve

To make the pancakes, sift the flour and salt into a bowl. Whisk in the eggs and milk. Cover with clingfilm and chill for 30 minutes.

To make the filling, peel and slice the banana and put into a large bowl. Pour over the lemon juice and stir gently until the banana is coated. Add the nectarines, mango, kiwi fruits and maple syrup and stir together gently until mixed.

Heat a little oil in a frying pan until hot. Remove the pancake batter from the refrigerator and add a large spoonful to the pan. Cook over a high heat until golden, then turn over and cook briefly on the other side. Remove from the pan and keep warm. Cook the other pancakes in the same way, stacking them on a plate. Keep warm. Divide the fruit filling between the pancakes and fold into triangles or roll into horns. Dust with icing sugar and serve with whipped cream.

Pear Crêpes with Chocolate Sauce

serves 4

crêpes

125 g/4½ oz plain flour

pinch of salt

3 eggs

250 ml/9 fl oz milk

2 tbsp lemon oil or vegetable oil

filling

250 g/9 oz dessert pears

8 cloves

3 tbsp currants

pinch of ground mixed spice

chocolate sauce

125 g/4½ oz plain chocolate, broken into small pieces

2½ tbsp butter

6 tbsp water

Preheat the oven to 160°C/325°F/Gas Mark 3.

To make the crêpes, sift the flour and salt into a bowl. Whisk in the eggs and milk to make a batter. Cover with clingfilm and chill for 30 minutes. Heat a little oil in a frying pan until hot. Add a large spoonful of the batter and cook over a high heat until golden, then turn over and cook briefly on the other side. Cook the other crêpes in the same way, stacking them on a plate.

To make the filling, bring a pan of water to the boil. Peel and slice the pears; add to the pan with the cloves and currants. Lower the heat and simmer for 5 minutes. Remove from the heat, drain, and discard the cloves. Leave to cool a little. Oil an ovenproof dish. Stir the mixed spice into the fruit; divide between the crêpes. Fold the crêpes into triangles. Arrange in the dish and bake for 15 minutes. To make the sauce, melt the chocolate and butter with the water in a small pan, stirring. Serve the crêpes with the sauce.

Grilled Honeyed Figs

serves 6

9 fresh figs, cut in half

4 tbsp clear honey

2 fresh rosemary sprigs, leaves removed and finely chopped (optional)

3 eggs

Preheat the grill to high. Arrange the figs, cut-side up, on the grill pan. Brush with half the honey and scatter over the rosemary, if using.

Cook under the preheated grill for 5–6 minutes, or until just beginning to caramelize.

Meanwhile, to make a sabayon, in a large, heatproof bowl, lightly whisk the eggs with the remaining honey, then place over a saucepan of simmering water. Using a hand-held electric whisk, beat the eggs and honey together for 10 minutes, or until pale and thick.

Put 3 fig halves in each of 6 bowls, add a generous spoonful of the sabayon and serve immediately.

Warm Currants in Cassis

serves 4

350 g/12 oz blackcurrants

225 g/8 oz redcurrants

4 tbsp caster sugar

grated rind and juice of
1 orange

2 tsp arrowroot

2 tbsp crème de cassis

whipped cream or fromage
frais, to serve

Using a fork, strip the blackcurrants and redcurrants from their stalks and put them in a pan.

Add the caster sugar and orange rind and juice and heat gently, stirring, until the sugar has dissolved. Bring to the boil and simmer gently for 5 minutes.

Drain the currants and place in a bowl, then return the juice to the pan.

Blend the arrowroot with a little water and mix into the juice in the pan. Boil the mixture until thickened.

Set aside to cool slightly, then stir in the crème de cassis.

Serve the currants in individual dishes with the juice and whipped cream or fromage frais.

Raspberry Brûlées

serves 4

250 g/9 oz raspberries

1 tbsp lemon juice

2 tbsp raspberry jam

125 ml/4 fl oz crème fraîche

125 ml/4 fl oz double
cream, lightly whipped

1 tsp vanilla essence

6 tbsp caster sugar

whole raspberries,
to decorate

Put the raspberries and lemon juice into a saucepan and stir over a low heat for about 5 minutes until they start to soften. Remove from the heat, stir in the jam, then divide between 4 ramekins.

Preheat the grill to hot. In a bowl, mix together the crème fraîche, cream and vanilla essence. Spoon the mixture over the raspberries and level the surfaces. Sprinkle the caster sugar over the top, allowing 1½ tablespoons per ramekin. Cook under the preheated grill, as close to the flames or element as possible, for 2–3 minutes, until the sugar caramelizes. Remove from the grill, decorate with whole raspberries and serve immediately.

Alternatively, to serve chilled, leave to cool to room temperature, then cover with clingfilm and place in the refrigerator to chill for 3–4 hours.

Banana Splits

serves 4

4 bananas

vanilla ice cream

300 ml/10 fl oz milk

1 tsp vanilla essence

3 egg yolks

100 g/3½ oz caster sugar

300 ml/10 fl oz double cream, whipped

chocolate rum sauce

125 g/4½ oz plain chocolate, broken into small pieces

2½ tbsp butter

6 tbsp water

1 tbsp rum

6 tbsp chopped mixed nuts, to decorate

To make the ice cream, heat the milk and vanilla essence in a saucepan until almost boiling. In a bowl, beat together the egg yolks and sugar. Remove the milk from the heat and stir a little into the egg mixture. Transfer the mixture to the pan. Stir over a low heat until thick, but do not boil. Remove from the heat. Cool for 30 minutes, fold in the cream, cover with clingfilm and chill for 1 hour. Transfer into an ice cream maker and process for 15 minutes. Alternatively, transfer into a freezerproof container and freeze for 1 hour, then place in a bowl and beat to break up the ice crystals. Put back in the container and freeze for 30 minutes. Repeat twice more, freezing for 30 minutes and whisking each time.

To make the sauce, melt the chocolate and butter with the water together in a saucepan, stirring. Remove from the heat and stir in the rum.

Peel the bananas, slice lengthways and arrange on 4 serving dishes. Top with ice cream and nuts and serve with the sauce.

Fresh Fruit Salad

serves 4

6 tbsp caster sugar

400 ml/14 fl oz water

½ tsp ground mixed spice

grated rind of ½ lemon

1 pawpaw

1 mango

1 pineapple

4 oranges, peeled and cut into segments

125 g/4½ oz strawberries, hulled and quartered

single or double cream, to serve (optional)

mint sprigs, to garnish

Place the sugar, water, mixed spice and lemon rind in a saucepan. Bring to the boil, stirring constantly, then continue to boil for 1 minute. Remove from the heat and leave to cool to room temperature. Transfer to a jug or bowl, cover with clingfilm and chill in the refrigerator for at least 1 hour.

Peel and halve the pawpaw and remove the seeds. Cut the flesh into small chunks or slices, and place in a large bowl. Cut the mango either side lengthways, close to the stone. Remove and discard the stone. Peel and cut the flesh into small chunks or slices, and add to the bowl. Cut off the top and bottom of the pineapple and remove the hard skin. Cut the pineapple in half lengthways, then into quarters, and remove the tough core. Cut the remaining flesh into small pieces and add to the bowl. Add the orange segments and strawberries. Pour over the chilled syrup, cover with clingfilm and chill until required.

Remove the fruit salad from the refrigerator and serve with single or double cream, if using, and garnish with mint sprigs.

Summer Pudding

serves 6

900 g/2 lb mixed berries, such as raspberries and blackberries

140 g/5 oz caster sugar

125 ml/4 fl oz milk

8 slices day-old white bread, crusts removed

Hull the berries and put them in a bowl. Sprinkle with the sugar and set aside.

Sprinkle the milk over the slices of bread to soften them slightly. Line the base and sides of a pudding basin with two thirds of the bread, cutting it to fit but overlap the edges slightly. Spoon the berries into the basin and place the remaining bread slices on top, cutting to fit and making sure that the fruit is completely covered.

Place a round of greaseproof paper on top of the last layer of bread. Put a plate or saucer, slightly smaller than the diameter of the basin, on top, then place a weight, such as a heavy can of fruit, on the plate. Leave to chill in the refrigerator for at least 8 hours.

To serve, remove the weight, plate and greaseproof paper. Invert a serving dish on top of the basin and, holding them together, reverse and shake sharply and the pudding should slide out. Serve immediately.

Upside-down Tropical Fruit Cake

serves 8

topping

55 g/2 oz butter, softened

55 g/2 oz light muscovado sugar

2 bananas

1 small pineapple

1 mango

cake

175 g/6 oz butter, softened, plus extra for greasing

175 g/6 oz light muscovado sugar

3 eggs

175 g/6 oz self-raising flour

1 tsp ground mixed spice

Preheat the oven to 180°C/350°F/Gas Mark 4. Grease a deep 20-cm/8-inch round cake tin.

To make the topping, spread the butter evenly over the base of the tin and sprinkle the sugar on top. Peel the bananas and slice thickly, then peel the pineapple and mango and cut into chunks. Mix the fruit together and pile evenly over the base of the tin.

To make the cake, place the butter, sugar and eggs in a bowl and sift in the flour and mixed spice. Beat together until light and fluffy, then spread the mixture over the fruit. Bake in the preheated oven for 1 hour, or until well risen and firm to the touch. Leave in the tin for 10 minutes, then loosen the edges with a palette knife and turn out onto a serving plate. Serve immediately.

Pavlova

serves 6

6 egg whites

pinch of cream of tartar

pinch of salt

275 g/9¾ oz caster sugar

600 ml/1 pint double cream

1 tsp vanilla essence

2 kiwi fruits, peeled and sliced

250 g/9 oz strawberries, hulled and sliced

3 ripe peaches, sliced

1 ripe mango, peeled and sliced

2 tbsp orange liqueur, such as Cointreau

fresh mint leaves, to decorate

Preheat the oven to 110°C/225°F/Gas Mark ¼. Line 3 baking trays with non-stick baking paper, then draw a 22-cm/8½-inch circle in the centre of each one. Beat the egg whites into stiff peaks. Mix in the cream of tartar and salt. Gradually add 200 g/7 oz of the sugar. Beat for 2 minutes until glossy. Fill a piping bag with the meringue mixture and pipe enough to fill each circle, doming them slightly in the centre. Bake for 3 hours. Remove from the oven. Leave to cool.

Whip together the cream and vanilla essence with the remaining sugar. Put the fruit into a separate bowl and stir in the liqueur. Put one meringue circle onto a plate, then spread over one third of the sugared cream. Spread over one third of the fruit, then top with a meringue circle. Spread over another third of cream, then another third of fruit. Top with the last meringue circle. Spread over the remaining cream, followed by the rest of the fruit. Decorate with mint leaves and serve.

Chocolate-dipped Fruit

serves 4

12 physalis
(Cape gooseberries)

200 g/7 oz plain chocolate,
broken into pieces

1 tbsp sunflower oil

12 small strawberries

Line a baking sheet with non-stick baking paper. Peel back the papery outer case from the physalis and twist at the top to make a 'handle'.

Put the chocolate and oil in a small, heatproof bowl, set the bowl over a saucepan of barely simmering water and heat until the chocolate has melted. Remove from the heat, stir and leave to cool until tepid.

Dip the fruit in the chocolate mixture and let any excess drain back into the saucepan. The fruit does not need to be completely coated.

Set the fruit on the prepared baking sheet. If the chocolate forms a 'foot' on the paper, it is too warm, so leave to cool slightly. If the chocolate in the bowl begins to set, warm it gently over the saucepan of simmering water. Chill the dipped fruit in the refrigerator for 30 minutes, or until the chocolate is set, then peel away from the paper. Serve on their own, or use to decorate another dessert.

Chilled
Desserts

Tiramisù

serves 4

200 ml/7 fl oz strong black coffee, cooled to room temperature

4 tbsp orange liqueur, such as Cointreau

3 tbsp orange juice

16 Italian sponge fingers

250 g/9 oz mascarpone cheese

300 ml/10 fl oz double cream, lightly whipped

3 tbsp icing sugar

grated rind of 1 orange

60 g/2¼ oz chocolate, grated

to decorate

chopped toasted almonds

crystallized orange peel

chocolate shavings

Pour the cooled coffee into a jug and stir in the orange liqueur and orange juice. Put 8 of the sponge fingers in the bottom of a serving dish, then pour over half of the coffee mixture.

Place the mascarpone cheese in a bowl with the cream, icing sugar and orange rind and mix together well. Spread half of the mascarpone mixture over the coffee-soaked sponge fingers, then arrange the remaining sponge fingers on top. Pour over the remaining coffee mixture and then spread over the remaining mascarpone mixture. Scatter over the grated chocolate and chill in the refrigerator for at least 2 hours. Serve decorated with chopped toasted almonds, crystallized orange peel and chocolate shavings.

Rich Chocolate Roulade

serves 4–6

cake

butter, for greasing

125 g/4½ oz dark chocolate, chopped

50 g/1¾ oz Continental plain chocolate, chopped

3 tbsp warm water

2 tbsp coffee-flavoured liqueur, such as Kahlúa (optional)

5 eggs, separated

175 g/6 oz caster sugar

filling

450 ml/16 fl oz double cream

40 g/1½ oz icing sugar, sifted, plus extra for dusting

20 g/¾ oz unsweetened cocoa powder

2 tsp espresso coffee powder, dissolved in 1 tbsp boiling water

fresh raspberries, to serve

Preheat the oven to 180°C/350°F/Gas Mark 4. Grease and line a 35 x 25-cm/14 x 10-inch Swiss roll tin.

Put the chocolate into a heatproof bowl and set over a saucepan of hot water, stirring occasionally, until melted. Stir in the water and liqueur, if using. Whisk the egg yolks and caster sugar in a bowl until pale. Beat the chocolate into the yolks. Whisk the egg whites in a clean bowl until stiff, then fold into the chocolate. Pour into the tin and bake for 15 minutes. Remove, cover with greaseproof paper and leave to cool for 3–4 hours. Meanwhile, whisk the filling ingredients together in a bowl until thick. Cover with clingfilm and chill.

Turn the cake out onto greaseproof paper dusted with icing sugar. Discard the lining paper. Reserve 4 tablespoons of the filling, then spread the rest over the roulade, leaving a 2.5-cm/1-inch border. Starting from a short side, roll up the cake. Discard the paper. Serve immediately with fresh raspberries.

Chocolate Cheesecake

serves 4–6

base

115 g/4 oz digestive biscuits, finely crushed

4 tbsp butter, melted, plus extra for greasing

2 tsp unsweetened cocoa powder

chocolate layer

800 g/1 lb 12 oz mascarpone cheese

200 g/7 oz icing sugar, sifted

juice of ½ orange

finely grated rind of 1 orange

175 g/6 oz plain chocolate, melted

2 tbsp brandy

chocolate leaves

12–16 firm, fresh, smooth non-toxic leaves, such as bay or citrus

175 g/6 oz plain chocolate, melted

halved kumquats, to decorate

Grease a 20-cm/8-inch loose-bottomed cake tin.

To make the base, place the crushed biscuits, cocoa powder and melted butter in a large bowl and mix well. Press the biscuit mixture evenly over the base of the prepared tin.

For the chocolate layer, place the mascarpone and icing sugar in a bowl and stir in the orange juice and rind. Add the melted chocolate and brandy, and mix together until thoroughly combined. Spread the chocolate mixture evenly over the biscuit layer. Cover with clingfilm and chill for at least 4 hours.

To make the chocolate leaves, wipe the leaves gently with kitchen paper. Using a pastry brush or clean paintbrush, carefully coat one side of each leaf with the melted chocolate, working from the centre to the edges. Do not let the chocolate run over the edges or onto the other side of the leaves, as it will make them almost impossible to remove without breaking the decoration. Place the leaves, coated side up, on a sheet of baking paper to set. When the chocolate has set, carefully peel away the leaves from the stalk ends, handling the chocolate leaves as little as possible.

Remove the cheesecake from the refrigerator, turn out onto a serving platter and decorate with the chocolate leaves and kumquat halves. Serve immediately.

Trifle

serves 4

fruit layer

6 trifle sponge cakes

2 tbsp strawberry jam

6 large strawberries, hulled and sliced

2 bananas, peeled and sliced

400 g/14 oz canned sliced peaches, drained

6 tbsp sherry

custard layer

250 ml/9 fl oz double cream

1 tsp vanilla essence

3 egg yolks

4 tbsp caster sugar

topping

300 ml/10 fl oz double cream

2 tbsp caster sugar

chopped mixed nuts, toasted, to decorate

To make the fruit layer, spread the sponge cakes with jam, cut into bite-sized pieces and arrange in the base of a glass serving bowl. Scatter over the fruit, pour over the sherry and set aside.

To make the custard, place the cream and vanilla essence in a saucepan and bring almost to the boil over a low heat. Meanwhile, place the egg yolks and sugar in a pudding basin and whisk together. Remove the cream mixture from the heat and gradually stir into the egg mixture. Return the mixture to the saucepan and warm over a low heat, stirring, until thickened. Remove the custard from the heat and leave to cool for 30 minutes, then pour it over the fruit layer. Cover with clingfilm and chill for 2½ hours.

Remove the trifle from the refrigerator. To make the topping, whip the cream and sugar together, then spread it evenly over the custard layer. Scatter the toasted, chopped mixed nuts over the top, then cover again with clingfilm and chill for a further 1½ hours. Serve chilled.

Crème Caramel

serves 4–6

butter, for greasing

175 g/6 oz plus 2 tbsp caster sugar

4 tbsp water

½ lemon

500 ml/18 fl oz milk

1 vanilla pod

2 large eggs

2 large egg yolks

fresh mint leaves, to decorate

Preheat the oven to 160°C/325°F/Gas Mark 3. Lightly grease the base and sides of two 600-ml/1-pint soufflé dishes. To make the caramel, place 75 g/2¾ oz sugar with the water in a saucepan over a medium-high heat and cook, stirring, until the sugar dissolves. Boil until the syrup turns a deep golden brown. Immediately remove from the heat and squeeze in a few drops of lemon juice. Divide evenly between the soufflé dishes and swirl around. Set aside.

Pour the milk into a saucepan. Slit the vanilla pod lengthways and add it to the milk. Bring to the boil, remove the saucepan from the heat and stir in the remaining sugar, stirring until it dissolves. Reserve.

Beat the eggs and egg yolks together in a bowl. Pour the milk mixture over them, whisking. Remove the vanilla pod. Strain the egg mixture into a bowl, then transfer and divide evenly between the soufflé dishes.

Place the dishes in a roasting tin with enough boiling water to come two thirds up the sides.

Bake in the preheated oven for 1–1¼ hours, or until a knife inserted in the centre comes out clean. Leave to cool completely. Cover with clingfilm and leave to chill for at least 24 hours.

Run a round-bladed knife around the edges of each dish. Place an up-turned serving plate with a rim on top, then invert the plate and dish, giving a sharp shake halfway over. Lift off the soufflé dishes and serve, decorated with fresh mint leaves.

Raspberries & Meringue Cream

serves 4

500 g/1 lb 2 oz raspberries

4 tbsp amaretto or crème de framboise liqueur

300 ml/10 fl oz double cream

6 small white meringues, coarsely crushed

Hull the raspberries, put them in a bowl and sprinkle the liqueur over them. Cover with clingfilm and leave to chill in the refrigerator for 2 hours.

Whip the cream in a large bowl until soft peaks form, then fold the raspberries, with their juices, into it. Sprinkle the crushed meringues on top and gently fold in. Spoon into a serving dish and serve immediately.

Blueberry Jelly with Cassis

serves 4–6

450 g/1 lb fresh blueberries, plus extra to decorate

150 ml/5 fl oz water

225 g/8 oz caster sugar

175 ml/6 fl oz crème de cassis

15 g/½ oz powdered gelatine

3 tbsp water

fresh mint leaves, to decorate

Put the blueberries, water and sugar in a saucepan and cook over a medium heat until softened.

Remove from the heat and leave to cool. Crush the berries with a wooden spoon to make a smooth purée.

Pour the purée into a measuring jug and add the cassis. Make up to 600 ml/1 pint, adding extra water if necessary.

Put the gelatine and the water in a heatproof cup and soak for 1–2 minutes until it is spongy. Put the cup in a small saucepan with enough water to come halfway up the sides, and heat over a low heat for 2–3 minutes until the gelatine has dissolved and the mixture is clear. Leave to cool until it is the same temperature as the fruit purée.

Mix the blueberry mixture and the gelatine together and pour into a jelly mould or a glass serving bowl. Cover with clingfilm and chill in the refrigerator until set. Serve decorated with fresh blueberries and mint leaves.

Cassata Semifreddo

serves 6–8

115 g/4 oz granulated sugar

150 ml/5 fl oz water

2 egg whites

50 g/1¾ oz chopped blanched almonds

50 g/1¾ oz mixed dried fruit

50 g/1¾ oz glacé cherries, chopped

300 ml/10 fl oz whipping cream

Line a 900-g/2-lb loaf tin or 1.4-litre/2½-pint oblong freezerproof plastic container with greaseproof paper, allowing it to hang over the edges of the container so that the cassata can be easily removed. Put the sugar and water in a small heavy-based saucepan and heat gently, stirring, until the sugar has dissolved. Bring to the boil, then boil, without stirring, for 5 minutes, or until a syrup has formed. Do not allow it to brown.

Meanwhile, whisk the egg whites until stiff and dry. Drizzle the hot syrup in a thin stream onto the whisked egg whites, whisking all the time until the mixture is thick, creamy and fluffy. Continue whisking until the mixture is cold.

Add the nuts, dried fruit and cherries to the meringue mixture and fold in until well blended. Whip the cream until it holds its shape, then fold in until well blended. Pour the mixture into the prepared tin or plastic container, cover and freeze for 5 hours, or until firm and cut into slices, using a hot knife.

To serve the cassata, uncover, stand the tin or plastic container in hot water for a few seconds to loosen it, then invert it onto a serving dish. Remove the greaseproof paper and, using a hot knife, cut into slices.

Biscuit Tortoni

serves 6

125 g/4 oz amaretti biscuits

300 ml/10 fl oz double cream

150 ml/5 fl oz single cream

115 g/4 oz icing sugar

4 tbsp Marsala

Line a 450-g/1-lb loaf tin or 850-ml/1½-pint oblong freezerproof plastic container with greaseproof paper, allowing it to hang over the edges of the container so that the tortoni can be easily removed. Put the biscuits in a food processor and process to form fine crumbs. Alternatively, put the biscuits in a strong polythene bag and crush with a rolling pin.

Pour the double cream and single cream into a large bowl and whip together until the mixture holds its shape. Sift the icing sugar into the whipped cream, then fold in the Marsala. Fold in two-thirds of the biscuits, reserving a third.

Pour the mixture into the prepared tin or plastic container, smooth the surface and freeze uncovered. If storing, cover the container with a lid.

Take the ice cream out of the freezer about 30 minutes before you are ready to serve it. Uncover, turn out onto a serving dish and remove the greaseproof paper. Leave at room temperature to soften slightly. Using a palette knife, press the reserved crushed biscuits lightly onto the top and sides of the ice cream until it is evenly coated. Serve cut into thick slices.

Chocolate Mousses

serves 4

300 g/10½ oz plain chocolate

1½ tbsp unsalted butter

1 tbsp brandy

4 eggs, separated

cocoa powder, for dusting

Break the chocolate into small pieces and place in a heatproof bowl set over a pan of simmering water. Add the butter and melt with the chocolate, stirring, until smooth. Remove from the heat, stir in the brandy and leave to cool slightly. Add the egg yolks and beat until smooth.

In a separate bowl, whisk the egg whites until stiff peaks have formed, then fold them into the chocolate mixture. Put 4 stainless steel cooking rings on 4 small serving plates, then spoon the mixture into the rings and level the surfaces. Transfer to the refrigerator and chill for at least 4 hours until set.

Take the mousses out of the refrigerator and remove the cooking rings. Dust with cocoa powder and serve.

Mascarpone Creams

serves 4

115 g/4 oz amaretti
biscuits, crushed

4 tbsp amaretto or
maraschino liqueur

4 eggs, separated

55 g/2 oz caster sugar

225 g/8 oz mascarpone
cheese

toasted flaked almonds,
to decorate

Place the amaretti crumbs in a bowl, add the amaretto or maraschino and set aside to soak.

Meanwhile, beat the egg yolks with the caster sugar until pale and thick. Fold in the mascarpone and soaked biscuit crumbs.

Whisk the egg whites in a separate, spotlessly clean, bowl until stiff, then gently fold into the cheese mixture. Divide the mascarpone cream among 4 serving dishes and chill for 1–2 hours. Sprinkle with toasted flaked almonds just before serving.

Apricot & Yogurt Cups

serves 4–6

600 ml/1 pint natural yogurt

few drops of almond extract

2–3 tsp clear honey, warmed

55 g/2 oz whole blanched almonds

175 g/6 oz ready-to-eat dried apricots

Line a 12-cup bun tin with small paper cake cases.

Spoon the yogurt into a mixing bowl, add the almond extract and honey and stir well. Using a small, sharp knife, cut the almonds into very thin slivers and stir into the yogurt mixture. Using a pair of kitchen scissors, cut the apricots into small pieces, then stir into the yogurt.

Spoon the mixture into the paper cases and freeze for 1½–2 hours, or until just frozen. Serve immediately.

Blueberry Fools

serves 4

25 g/1 oz custard powder

300 ml/10 fl oz skimmed or semi-skimmed milk

2 tbsp caster sugar

150 g/5½ oz fresh or frozen blueberries, thawed if frozen

200 g/7 oz low-fat natural fromage frais

Blend the custard powder with 50 ml/2 fl oz of the milk in a heatproof bowl. Bring the remaining milk to the boil in a small saucepan and pour over the custard mixture, mixing well. Return the custard to the saucepan and bring to the boil over a medium-low heat, stirring constantly, until thickened. Pour the custard into the bowl and sprinkle the sugar over the top of the custard to prevent a skin forming. Cover and leave to cool completely.

Reserve 12 blueberries for decoration. Put the remaining blueberries and the cold custard into a blender and blend until smooth.

Spoon the fromage frais and the blueberry mixture in alternate layers into 4 tall glasses. Decorate with the reserved blueberries and serve immediately.

Layered Nectarine Cream

serves 4

4 nectarines, peeled, stoned and sliced

2 tbsp amaretto liqueur

175 g/6 oz curd cheese

300 ml/10 fl oz peach-flavoured yogurt

Reserve a few nectarine slices for decoration. Put the remainder in a bowl, add the liqueur and toss gently, then set aside.

Beat the cheese and yogurt together in another bowl until thoroughly combined. Spoon half the mixture into 4 tall glasses. Divide the nectarine and liqueur mixture among them and top with the remaining cheese and yogurt mixture.

Decorate with the reserved nectarine slices and leave to chill in the refrigerator for at least 30 minutes before serving.

Rich Vanilla Ice Cream

serves 4–6

300 ml/10 fl oz single cream and 300 ml/ 10 fl oz double cream or 600 ml/1 pint whipping cream

1 vanilla pod

4 large egg yolks

115 g/4 oz caster sugar

Pour the single and double cream or the whipping cream into a large heavy-based saucepan. Split open the vanilla pod and scrape out the seeds into the cream, then add the whole vanilla pod too. Bring almost to the boil, then remove from the heat and leave to infuse for 30 minutes.

Put the egg yolks and sugar in a large bowl and whisk together until pale and the mixture leaves a trail when the whisk is lifted. Remove the vanilla pod from the cream, then slowly add the cream to the egg mixture, stirring all the time with a wooden spoon. Strain the mixture into the rinsed-out saucepan or a double boiler and cook over a low heat for 10–15 minutes, stirring all the time, until the mixture thickens enough to coat the back of the spoon. Do not allow the mixture to boil or it will curdle. Remove the custard from the heat and leave to cool for at least 1 hour, stirring from time to time to prevent a skin from forming.

If using an ice cream machine, churn the cold custard in the machine following the manufacturer's instructions. Alternatively, freeze the custard in a freezerproof container, uncovered, for 1–2 hours, or until it begins to set around the edges. Turn the custard into a bowl and stir with a fork or beat in a food processor until smooth. Return to the freezer and freeze for a further 2–3 hours, or until firm. Cover the container with a lid for storing.

Dark & White Chocolate Ice Cream

serves 4

6 egg yolks

100 g/3½ oz caster sugar

350 ml/12 fl oz milk

175 ml/6 fl oz double cream

100 g/3½ oz dark chocolate, chopped

75 g/2¾ oz white chocolate, grated or finely chopped

fresh mint leaves, to decorate

Place the egg yolks and sugar in a heatproof bowl and beat until fluffy. Heat the milk, cream and dark chocolate in a saucepan over a low heat, stirring, until melted and almost boiling. Remove from the heat and whisk into the egg mixture. Return the mixture to the pan and cook, stirring, over a low heat until thick. Do not let it simmer. Transfer to a heatproof bowl and cool. Cover with clingfilm and chill for 1½ hours. Remove from the refrigerator and stir in the white chocolate.

Transfer to a freezerproof container and freeze for 1 hour. Remove from the freezer, transfer to a bowl and whisk to break up the ice crystals. Return to the container and freeze for 30 minutes. Repeat twice more, freezing for 30 minutes and whisking each time. Alternatively, transfer the mixture to an ice cream machine and process for 15 minutes.

Scoop the ice cream into serving bowls, decorate with mint leaves and serve.

Mango Sorbet

serves 4–6

2 large ripe mangoes

juice of 1 lemon

pinch of salt

115 g/4 oz sugar

3 tbsp water

Using a sharp knife, thinly peel the mangoes, holding them over a bowl to catch the juices. Cut the flesh away from the central stone and put in a food processor or blender. Add the mango juice, lemon juice and salt and process to form a smooth purée. Push the mango purée through a nylon sieve into a bowl.

Put the sugar and water in a heavy-based saucepan and heat gently, stirring, until the sugar has dissolved. Bring to the boil, without stirring, then remove from the heat and leave to cool slightly.

Pour the syrup into the mango purée and mix well together. Leave to cool, then chill the mango syrup in the refrigerator for 2 hours, or until cold.

If using an ice cream machine, churn the mixture in the machine following the manufacturer's instructions. Alternatively, freeze the mixture in a freezerproof container, uncovered, for 3–4 hours, or until mushy. Turn the mixture into a bowl and stir with a fork or beat in a food processor to break down the ice crystals. Return to the freezer and freeze for a further 3–4 hours, or until firm. Cover the container with a lid for storing.

Citrus Granita

serves 6

6 oranges

1½ lemons

140 g/5 oz sugar

450 ml/16 fl oz water

6 amaretti biscuits, to serve

Pare the rind from the fruit, cut off and discard the pith, then slice a few thin strips of rind and reserve them separately from the large pieces. Squeeze the juice from the fruit.

Boil the sugar and water in a heavy-based saucepan and stir until the sugar dissolves. Boil, without stirring, for 10 minutes until syrupy. Remove from the heat, stir in the large rind pieces, cover and leave to cool.

Strain the cooled syrup into a freezerproof container and stir in the juice. Freeze, uncovered, for 4 hours until slushy.

Blanch the thin rind strips in a saucepan of boiling water for 2 minutes. Drain and refresh with cold water. Pat dry with kitchen paper.

Remove the granita from the freezer and break up with a fork. Freeze again for a further 4 hours, or until hard.

Remove the granita from the freezer and leave until slightly softened. Beat with a fork, then spoon into glasses and decorate with the rind strips. Serve with the biscuits.